CARS

by Bob Ottum

illustrated by William Dugan

A GOLDEN BOOK • NEW YORK

Western Publishing Company, Inc.
Racine, Wisconsin 53404

Cars come in many shapes and sizes, just as people do. Great big people often drive great big cars. Small people often drive small cars.

But not always.

Large families usually have extra-big cars called station wagons or vans, with plenty of room for children and dogs and toys and things. Small families sometimes have small cars called compact cars.

But not always.

Cars come in different colors, too. There are plain black cars. There are plain white cars. There are bright-colored cars and cars with two different colors.

Some cars have *lots* of different colors!

Cars take people to work every day. Sometimes people who work at the same place take turns driving and giving the others a ride.

Some people work right in their cars.

Cars take people shopping for groceries and clothes and furniture and other things. If something is too big to fit in the backseat, it goes in the trunk of the car. Sometimes it goes on top of the car.

BUS
STOP

Cars even take people shopping for other cars.
At this car lot, there are brand-new cars and used
cars, too, for sale.

Some people like to drive very old cars. This car can't travel fast, but it's been going for a long, long time!

Cars take people on vacations. Some people go to the desert in their car. Some people go to the mountains.

Some people even go across a lake in their car!

Racing cars are special cars that go very fast. They are driven only on special roads, and lots of people come to watch. Which car will win this race?

This funny-looking car goes very, *very* fast. It goes so fast it almost flies. It even has a parachute to help it stop!

Cars are important. Many people use cars to get wherever they're going.

But . . . not always!